W9-CCJ-651

# VE DAY
## in Photographs

# VE DAY
## in Photographs

Sean McKnight

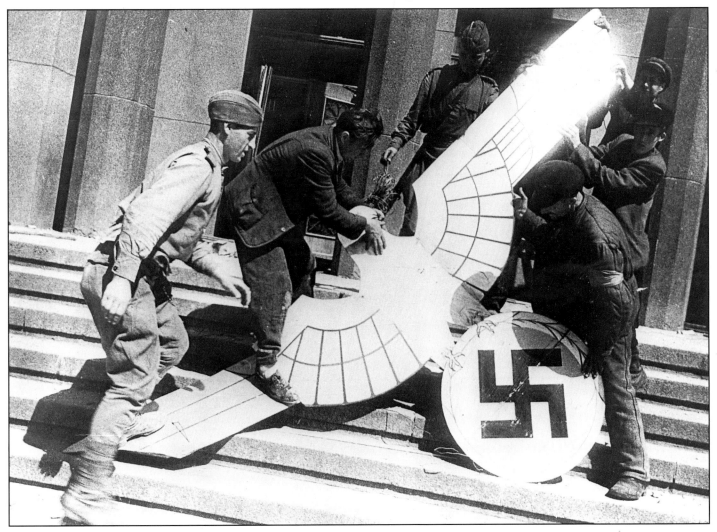

a Salamander book

**Published by Salamander Books Limited**
LONDON

# A SALAMANDER BOOK

Distributed by Random House Value Publishing, Inc.
40 Engelhard Avenue
Avenel, New Jersey 07001

A CIP catalog record for this book is available from the Library of Congress.

Printed in Belgium

© Salamander Books Ltd 1995

ISBN 0-517-12156-5

All rights reserved. No part of this book may be reproduced, stored in a retrieval system or transmitted in any form or by any means, electronic, mechanical, photocopying, recording or otherwise, without the prior permission of Salamander Books Ltd.

All correspondence concerning the content of this volume should be addressed to Salamander Books Ltd, 129-137 York Way, London N7 9LG, United Kingdom.

PICTURE CREDITS
The publishers wish to thank the following picture agencies and archives for supplying the photographs in this book. Sources are credited by page number.

Front cover: Popperfoto; Back cover, Top: Range/Bettmann; Center, Popperfoto; Bottom: US National Archives, Washington, DC (USNA); Page 1: Imperial War Museum (IWM); 2-3: Novosti Photo Library, London (NOV); 4-5: Hulton Deutsch; 6-7: Range/Bettmann/UPI; 8-9: NOV (all); 10: IWM; 112: NOV (all); 12: Above, Hulton Deutsch; Left, Popperfoto; 13: Hulton Deutsch; 14: Above, Hulton Deutsch; Left, Popperfoto; 15: Above, Popperfoto; Right, Hulton Deutsch; 16: Popperfoto (all); 17: Right, Popperfoto; Below, Hulton Deutsch; 18: Above, Popperfoto; Left, Hulton Deutsch; 19: Above, Popperfoto; Right, USNA; 20: Popperfoto; 21: Popperfoto (all); 22: Hulton Deutsch (all); 23: Range/Bettmann; 24-25: Left, Hulton Deutsch; Center, Range/Bettmann/UPI; Right, Range/Bettmann; 26: Range/Bettmann; 27: Left, Hulton Deutsch; Below left, Range/Bettmann; 28: Range/Bettmann/UPI; 29: Above, USNA; Left, Range/Bettmann; 30: USNA; 31: Hulton Deutsch (all); 32-33: IWM, (all); 34-35: IWM, (all); 36: IWM (all); 37: Above, IWM; Left, Hulton Deutsch; 38-39: NOV (all); 40: Right, IWM; Below right, NOV; 41: IWM; 42-43: NOV (all); 44-45: USNA; 46: Above, NOV; Right, IWM; 47: IWM; 48: IWM (all); 49: Hulton Deutsch; 50: IWM (all); 51: Right, Hulton Deutsch; Below, Range/Bettmann/UPI; 52: Above, NOV; 53: IWM (all); 54-55: NOV; 56-57: NOV (all); 58-59: IWM (all); 60-61: IWM (all); 62-63: NOV (all); 64: IWM.

CREDITS
Editor: Tony Hall
Designer: Paul Johnson
Filmset: SX Composing Ltd, England
Color and mono reproduction:
P&W Graphics PTE Ltd, Singapore

9 8 7 6 5 4 3 2 1

Prelim captions: Page 1/Half title: VE Day in the Belgian capital, Brussels. Pages 2-3/Title: Dismantling the symbols of tyranny; the Reichstag in Berlin, May 1945. Pages 4-5/Contents: VE-Day in London.

# CONTENTS

# Chapter 1

# VICTORY DAYS

Right: The crowd filling Times Square on May 7, 1945 celebrates the end of the war in Europe. The joy of New Yorkers, however, was slightly premature. Germany formally surrendered in Berlin on the following day. Fighting, however, continued to the 9th when the Soviet Red Army won control of the Czech capital, Prague.

Left: The Allied armies from East and West met on the River Elbe, which the American Ninth Army reached on April 11. This meeting of allies was a moment for celebration, but also a time for scoring propaganda points. Here the Red Army are making a subtle point, playing cordial "host" to the American "guest".

*Our Greating to the heroes army of United States of America*

Below: A GI of the 68th Infantry Division strikes a light for his new Red Army friend. Encountering US troops was a bonus for Soviet forces. American rations – and generosity – provided a welcome break from the somewhat basic Red Army rations.

Right: Both Americans and Soviets played up their meeting for the cameras. On both sides there was a friendly interest and curiosity but the Soviet authorities, traditionally suspicious of contact with foreigners, rarely permitted unsupervised fraternization with their capitalist allies.

Left: Field Marshal Montgomery, second on the right, discusses surrender terms with representatives of German forces in Northwestern Germany, the Netherlands and Denmark. The Germans were anxious to avoid surrendering to the Soviets, but Montgomery, quite correctly, declined to accept the surrender of three German Armies facing the Russians in the east. Following this meeting, hostilities in this theatre of war ceased at 8.00 a.m. on May 4.

Below: General Jodl signing the instrument of surrender at General Eisenhower's SHAEF HQ in Reims, France on May 7. Ending a war fought on the scale of World War II was not a simple matter, and in reality the process of the German surrender consisted of various agreements – both local and general – spread over several days.

Above: The Soviets insisted that the formal act of German surrender be signed in Berlin, and the photograph shows Allied military delegates proceeding to the ceremony. This unconditional surrender on May 8 meant that the German nation surrendered directly to the USSR – the power which had done more than any other to defeat Nazi Germany.

Right: Field Marshal Keitel signs the formal act proclaiming the unconditional surrender of Germany. Many of Keitel's fellow officers regarded him as an over-zealous servant of the Nazi regime – his nickname was Lach Keitel (lackey Keitel); he paid for his complicity with the regime by being sentenced to death at the Nuremberg trials held later the same year (see page 54).

Above: As news of the surrender spread, so crowds assembled around many of London's famous landmarks; including Piccadilly Circus. Clearly some of these celebrants had an eye for the right sort of transport. Judging from the passenger's faces they have already sampled the excellent Toby Ale they are helping on its way.

Left: An American soldier reads reports of the German surrender in the London Evening News. There were 3,072,540 American military personnel in Northwest Europe in May 1945, and for most of these Britain had become a second home. Within a couple of years the American armed forces would return for an even longer stay in Europe, but in 1945 few Americans anticipated the onset of the Cold War.

Right: Canadian troops entertain the crowds in Leicester Square while waiting for the speech by King George VI. The Canadians had been belligerents since 1939, and 217,421 Canadian servicemen participated in the invasion of Germany. In the Northwest European campaign alone, Canada suffered 43,892 casualties, a high price for a small nation to pay for its commitment to democracy and its loyalty to Britain.

Below: The ticker-tape shows the location of these celebrants to be near London's Fleet Street. Two lucky sailors celebrate VE Day surrounded by women office workers. Women had constituted a minority of office workers before 1939, but the war significantly accelerated the trend towards employing women.

Above: In London, news of the end of the war against Germany sparked off wild celebrations. The Star Spangled Banner was almost as ubiquitous as the Union Jack – a comment on the depth of Anglo-American wartime co-operation and friendship.

Left: Behind a collection of beer glasses – beer was one of the few consumer goods not to be rationed in wartime Britain – a couple kiss.

Above: Watched by commuters queuing for a bus near Leicester Square, celebrants dance in the street. It looks as though the gentleman in the suit is not keen on his lady friend dancing with a cheerful sergeant, but on VE Day wearing a uniform was a passport to all sorts of VIP treatment.

Right: A crowd lives it up in Piccadilly Circus; still without the statue of Eros, which had been kept safely stored away from German bombs. For the British people VE Day was a well deserved culmination to years of struggle. Britain had made a total effort during the war, but the euphoria of victory was to be followed by the need to rebuild an exhausted economy.

Left: A British-made lorry in Parliament Square demonstrates its robust qualities for the camera. Celebrating besides the ''Mother of Parliaments'' was highly appropriate, many Western Allied servicemen – especially Americans – having seen the war as a crusade for democracy against dictatorship.

Below: The crowd in Whitehall, having listened to Prime Minister Winston Churchill's speech at 3.00 p.m., get into party mood. Churchill was a popular hero with the British people, but his personal standing did not extend to the Conservative Party, which was comprehensively defeated by the Labour Party in the July 1945 General Election.

Right and below: The Royal Family and Prime Minister Winston Churchill on the balcony of Buckingham Palace, acknowledge the cheering of the large crowd. The British monarchy – not universally popular in the early stages of the war – had emerged from the conflict a stronger popular institution; ordinary people felt they had shared the burdens of war, and the appearance of the future Queen Elizabeth II (bottom far left) in uniform symbolised a common, national purpose.

Above: Land girls in a cheerful mood in Trafalgar Square. In 1945, 65,000 women were members of the Women's Land Army, and in total there were 204,000 women working on the land. During the war they had released men from agricultural work, and helped to substantially boost Britain's food production.

Left: As the partying continued it seems as though demobilisation was taking place as the camera clicked – at least the uniforms were disappearing from their official owners. British servicemen in reality faced a gradual process of demobilisation, avoiding the social problems caused by a rapid return to "Civvy Street" like those that had occurred in 1918; in contrast, the United States demobilised very rapidly.

Above: The Palace of Westminster, blazing with lights, declares to Londoners that the long nights of blackout are over. The British authorities expected bombing to cause dreadful casualties, but the 60,000 deaths inflicted by German bombing – a tragic enough statistic – was well below the most "optimistic" prediction of experts in 1939.

Right: Clearly the spirit of entrepreneurship had not died – despite the politically controlled "Command Economy" adopted in wartime Britain. Captured here, a rather smart suitcase salesman sells 2nd lieutenants Betty Pat and Irma Iannitell (US Army nurses) hats that complement their uniforms perfectly for the nights partying.

Above: The children of Sutton Dwellings in
Chelsea, London, have a cause to celebrate.
Clearly more than a few ration books have
been exhausted to provide this feast.
However, post-war Britain remained an
austere society, and sweets and chocolates
remained rationed into the 1950s.

Above: Children could look forward to a better future as a result of a newly-forged determination, not to return to the hardships of the 1930s. Full employment, a universal health service and access to a decent education were all commitments made good by Britain's post-war Labour Government.

Below: All over Britain flags went up for VE Day street parties. World War II was a time of hardship and tragedy for the British people, but it was also a time of striving for a common enterprise. The war helped sweep away much that was divisive in British society.

Above: For Britain, her second world conflict in fifty years marked an end to imperial grandeur. Britain's cumulative debt stood at £16 billion in 1945, and the awakening nationalism of the colonies and dependencies ensured that within 30 years the sun would have set on the British Empire.

Above: In Washington DC an ebullient
President Harry S. Truman reads to the press
the text of his radio broadcast to the
American people, in which he announced
Germany's unconditional surrender. Truman
had become president following the death in
office of Franklin Delano Roosevelt on April
12, but – despite his relative unfamiliarity
with international politics – he was soon
setting a new combative tone in dealing with
the Soviet Union.

Right: In contrast to London, there are no
uniforms apparent in this New York crowd
scene. During the war the US had managed
to field the world's second largest army, as
well as the most powerful air force and naval
fleet, without fully mobilising her economy
for war.

Above: New York's Wall Street had reasons
to celebrate; the war had galvanised the US
economy (average real earnings had risen by
70 per cent since 1941). Despite some fears of
a return to the 1930s, the growth of the
American economy continued after 1945.

Above: Two British sailors and a cheerful American soldier celebrate the end of the war in Europe. The USA had been a silent partner in the battle of the Atlantic even before they joined the war against Germany in 1941, and many British seamen had found New York a welcoming port of call.

Above: Flags deck this Chicago department store, those of the other Allies symbolically dwarfed by the Star Spangled Banner. The "Lend-Lease" scheme demonstrated the USA's massive wartime resources, a total of $48 billion being "loaned" to America's allies. A victorious United States emerged from World War II in an unparalleled position of global eminence.

Above: For the important New York Jewish community the end of the war was a joy, but the emerging details of the Nazi's Final Solution - the planned extermination of European Jewry – were to cause profound shock. Sympathy for the victims of the Holocaust made the United States extremely sympathetic to Zionist aspirations to found a Jewish state.

# VE-DAY

Right: An excellent way to celebrate the end of the war, but on both sides of the Atlantic the war had stimulated very different attitudes to married life, and sexual mores. In California, Los Angeles County alone registered nearly 18,000 divorces in 1944.

Left: The ticker-tape streams down, but behind the crowds the posters warn that Japan has yet to be beaten. There was a powerful group in the USA that had always seen the Pacific war as America's main task, not least amongst their motives being a desire for vengeance against the Japanese for their infamous attack on Pearl Harbor in December 1941.

Left: The festivities continued late into the evening, but it seems as though these particular party goers have already drunk their fill. Thank goodness for a well lubricated VE Day that America had abandoned prohibition in 1933.

# VE-DAY

Below: The model of the statue of Liberty looms over the crowds in Times Square, New York. Although America no longer accepted all immigrants, survivors of the war in Europe looked principally to the USA for material help in rebuilding their shattered societies.

EMBASSY NEWSREE

OFFICIAL ARMY SIGNAL CORPS FILMS **NAZI ATROCITIES** OHRD HADA NORDHA BUCHEN

HELD OVER! MAIDANEK "NAZI DEATH FACTORY" SEE S.S. GUARDS EXECUTED

Above: The war left a dreadful legacy of violations against the human spirit, and American audiences – many of whom dismissed accounts of extermination camps as fanciful – required the evidence of their own eyes to believe the depths to which a "civilized" nation could stoop.

Left: The Churchillian "V" for victory is made by many in this crowd, but the flags are all American. In 1945 Americans hoped for a better world, based on many of the values which they believed had made the United States thrive. One of the causes of the Cold War was an inability of many Americans to appreciate why the USSR was unwilling to participate in their world vision.

Above: Paris, lit up on the evening of May 8, emerged from the war with relatively little physical damage. This owed much to the German commander of the greater Paris region, General von Choltitz, who in August 1944 refused to execute Hitler's orders to conduct a Stalingrad like defence, and to wantonly destroy large sections of the city.

Above: The crowd in the Palace de l'Opera, in Paris, blithely ignoring the traffic sign, celebrate the German surrender. It is often forgotten that the French provided an important component of the Allied forces in the 1944-45 Northwest Europe campaign: by the end of the war 437,144 French servicemen were participants in the invasion of Germany.

Below: These French women, charmingly sporting the "colours" of the Grand Alliance, suggest that a liberated France has returned to the front rank of nations. The striking hammer and sickle designer number should remind us that post-war Europe moved politically to the left. In the French elections of 1948 the French Communists won more votes than any other party.

Above: This bustling Belgian street scene is deceptive; liberated Western Europe was not to recover substantially until the United States lent a helping hand. It took the 1948 Marshall Plan to ''prime the pump'' of the European economy. By 1952 the Americans had given credits of nearly $13 billion to Western Europe.

Right: Members of the British Army's Royal Army Ordnance Corps (RAOC) enjoying VE Day in the Belgium capital, Brussels. By the end of the war nearly 900,000 tons (914,000 tonnes) of supplies a month were pouring into Belgian ports, and the RAOC played a vital role in the logistic chain sustaining the Allied 21st and 12th Army Groups.

Above: Crowds listen to an American military band – no doubt playing some of the jazz music, which Hitler had dismissed as degenerate - in the medieval magnificence of the Grande Place in Brussels. Brussels had been spared the horrors of prolonged street fighting by the speed with which the British had liberated the city in September 1944.

Left: Allied soldiers dance with Belgian civilians celebrating the end of the war. Although Belgium was better off than its neighbours, only an Allied airlift had averted a winter food shortage. This led to post-liberation discontent and the fall of the Belgian government in February 1946.

Above: VE Day in the Netherlands was both
a celebration and a liberation for many
Dutch. The bulk of the province of Holland
remained under German control until the
war's end; an occupation that ended only
when German forces surrendered to
Montgomery's 21st Army Group.

Right: The Dutch resistance had flared into
action in the autumn of 1944, and Dutch
railway workers began a general strike
which, despite executions of strike leaders,
lasted to the end of the war. The Germans
punished the increasingly restive Dutch by
reducing food supplies, and by May 1945 a
working man's daily ration rarely exceeded
500 calories. Despite the joy of the war in
Europe ending, the country was perilously
close to starvation.

Right: A clear demonstration of the
egalitarianism of the British Army at war,
both the sergeant, and the commissioned
officer, reap the rewards of being a liberator.

Below: The British officers on the balcony
were no doubt especially welcomed by this
Dutch crowd in the town of Enschede.
Between April 29 and May 8 the Allies –
mainly the RAF – had flown in 10,850 tons
(11,000 tonnes) of food and supplies.

Above: Free Danish troops clearly delighted to meet British soldiers in Copenhagen. Since January 1945 the Danish "secret army", under the command of General Gortz, had been very active in co-operating with the Western Allies.

Below: The Allies feared that Soviet paratroopers might get to Copenhagen first. Chaos on the roads was delaying 21st Army Group's armoured spearheads, but General Dewing flew in a company of British 1st Airborne Division in 12 Dakota aircraft.

Above: British forces liberated Norway without any fighting, following the surrender of the German occupying forces on May 5. A minority of Norwegians had supported the pro-German government of Vidkun Quisling, but German occupation, and the brutal response to the Norwegian resistance movement, ensured the arrival of elements of the British 1st Airborne was a moment to celebrate.

Left: In Oslo, Norwegians greet Crown Prince Olaf on his return home from Great Britain. The Norwegian royal family firmly identified with the anti-Nazi cause, continuing their resistance to the German invasion from exile.

Above: A Red Army T-34 moves along a
street in the Czechoslovak capital, Prague; it
is probably part of the Fourth Guards Army
which led the way into the city. The situation
in Czechoslovakia was very confused;
General Vlasov's army of anti-Bolshevik
Russians, hitherto fighting for the Germans,
switched sides and began to help local units
of the Czech resistance take control of most
of Prague – though resistance leaders angrily
repudiated these unwelcome new allies.
Despite the hopes of some Czechs, the
Soviets insisted that their forces, and not the
Americans, liberate the Czech capital.

Above: The Kremlin and St. Basil's Cathedral overlook the crowd, symbolising how in the desperate days of 1941 the Communist regime had evoked the pre-revolutionary past. The "Great Patriotic War" was fought with the blessings of the Orthodox Church, and Peter the Great ranked with Lenin as an inspirational figure from the past.

Below: Leningrad withstood a 28 month siege, and its celebrations at the end of the war were heartfelt. Nearly one million inhabitants were evacuated in 1942, over 200,000 were killed by bombardment, and 633,000 died from starvation: by then more people had died in the city than in the USA and the UK combined.

# Chapter 2

# GOING HOME

Right: Members of a US Army Medium Automobile Maintenance Ordnance Company celebrate VE Day with "liberated" German beer. It was the Western Allied forces, not the Germans, who possessed the real mechanised armies of World War II. Units such as this one – no doubt already looking forward to getting home – had kept those armies on the move.

Above: These British prisoners of war are on their way home, having been freed by the Red Army near Berlin. On the whole the Germans had treated Western POWs in reasonable accordance with the Geneva Conventions, but despite this, life in the Stalags was bleak, and very dull.

Right: These soldiers were lucky, liberation by the US Ninth Army meant rapid repatriation and access to the finest rations of any Allied army. The scene reveals a mixture of troops from the British Commonwealth and Empire; the Sikh in his distinctive turban is probably a member of the Indian Army (in 1945, about 2 million strong).

Below: The British POWs in Stalag 79 were liberated by the Red Army, but having been temporarily unable to get back home, they used what the Germans had left behind to turn their old prison into more comfortable accommodation. In the chaos of Europe in 1945 some POWs waited months for repatriation.

Above: These soldiers were amongst the first British troops to be demobilised. Not before time too for Private Bill Krepper of the Pioneer Corps (second right). Bill was 55 years old, and he served from May 1940 to 1945; this on top of four years with the Northumberland Fusiliers during World War I.

Right: Ex-Private Krepper, being fitted with his de-mob suit at the Olympia Clothing Centre in London. For many ordinary people these suits would be their "best wear" for years. For most people clothing remained the basic "utility" style, post-war Britain being bedeviled by shortages. The utility grade of clothing had been introduced in 1941, under Board of Trade supervision, to guarantee an acceptable standard using minimal resources.

Above: In 1945, Britain faced an acute shortage of housing. Half a million homes had been destroyed by bombs, but the virtual suspension of wartime building meant that the shortage was officially estimated as 1.25 million. The photograph shows a "prefab" – homes that could be constructed quickly filling the housing gap – one of over 150,000 built by 1948. Despite the Labour Government subsidizing the building of 1.25 million homes by 1951, the prefabs remained in use far longer than anticipated; indeed, some people claimed to prefer their prefabs to more conventional housing.

Above: The liner *Queen Elizabeth* arriving in New York's magnificent natural harbour. The river boat meeting the liner is full of members of the Women's Auxiliary Army Corps, who carried gifts with them for the returning veterans.

Right: Wearing their distinctive flying jackets, these US airmen are travelling home in style on the liner *Queen Elizabeth*. Only the very best recruits had been selected for aircrew, but the stresses faced by these men were immense; 79,265 American airmen died on bombing raids during the war.

Right: Despite returning home on crutches this serviceman is greeted with joy by his family. Compared to its allies, the United States had suffered fewer casualties overall. However, 124,960 American servicemen gave their lives in the 1944-45 Northwest European campaign – nearly two-thirds of all the Western Allied casualties. The American government showed its gratitude for the sacrifices of its veterans by enacting the GI Bill of Rights, which provided them with money to go to college, and access to subsidised mortgages.

Below: These are some of the first batch of 4,381 US servicemen to arrive back home after VE-Day. On arrival in New York City they were greeted by the Embarkation Special Service Division of entertainers. Many returning troops were earmarked not for demobilisation but for the Pacific war. Only after Japan surrendered in August did demobilisation get properly underway, with 150,000 Americans a month leaving the service.

Above: A field of rubble is all that remained
of the Soviet village of Melnitsa – destroyed
by the Nazis in 1942. It is hard to appreciate
the sheer scale of the devastation of the war
in the East. The USSR had lost over a quarter
of its pre-war wealth and 25 million Soviet
citizens were homeless.

Top right: The homecomings were not just reserved for servicemen. Gustaaf De Sadeleer embraces his wife for the first time in 5 years. Along with thousands of other Belgian workers, he had spent the war in Germany as a slave labourer. He was one of the luckier victims, most of the 5 million forced to work for the Third Reich never returned.

Right: Europe in the spring of 1945 was full of huge numbers of refugees – approximately 25 million of them. Some fled in the path of the Red Army, others were just left by their German captors, many wandered searching for a roof over their heads. Many were ethnic Germans ejected from the restored Slavic states of Eastern Europe.

# Chapter 3

# UNFINISHED BUSINESS

Right: The accused in the dock at the war crimes trials in Nuremberg, Germany – Wilhelm Keitel stands before the judges. Before the war ended, the Allies had already begun to consider what the fate of the defeated Germans should be. Some Americans favoured the Morgenthau Plan – which envisaged the total destruction of Germany's industrial base – and in both the USSR and Britain there was talk of savage retribution. The decision to put the Nazi leaders on trial instead, and to treat the German people as more victims than perpetrators was a tribute to the nobler instincts of the Grand Alliance.

Above: It did not take the Soviets long to realise that they needed to rebuild their occupation zone, and these Germans are clearing the Berlin underground railway system. The task of reconstructing Germany was colossal, by May 1945, 3.37 million German homes had been destroyed and 7.5 million Germans were homeless.

Below: Millions of Germans had fled west, fearing the treatment the Red Army would mete out to them, not without reason, for the invading Soviet forces were responsible for numerous atrocities against civilians. However, despite the Soviets initially looting factories, the Red Army found themselves keeping their ex-enemies alive.

Above: In Berlin, the magnificent Brandenburg Gate, on the right, was too solid a structure to easily destroy, but few buildings in the city survived in this good a condition. Despite their hopeless situation, the Germans had fought desperately for their capital, and in the 17-day battle for the city the Soviets had suffered 352,475 casualties.

Below: From left to right Marshal Zhukov, General Eisenhower and Field Marshal Montgomery at the formal start of the German occupation. As had previously been agreed at the Allied conference in Yalta, the Allied military leaders set up an Allied Control Commission to co-ordinate the administration of their zones of control.

Above: Hitler committed suicide on April 30, but feeling betrayed by both Himmler and Goering, he passed what remained of his power to Grand Admiral Doenitz. The government that presided over the final death throes of the Third Reich was a mixture of military men, lesser Nazi functionaries and right wing conservatives. Despite the new government's complicity with the Nazi regime many of its members were surprised, and angry, when men of the British Cheshire Regiment placed them in custody on May 23.

Left: Grand Admiral Doenitz (sitting to the left of the man standing), and the members of his government on their way to captivity in Britain. Doenitz was tried for war crimes at Nuremberg, where he argued that during the war he was doing no more than his duty. Many British and American naval officers seem to have agreed, and several testified that the unrestricted U-Boat campaign he masterminded was similar to that waged by the Allies against Japan.

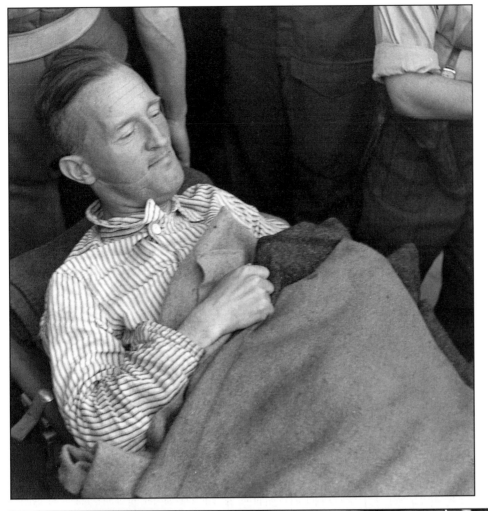

Left: In the chaos of defeated Germany many top Nazis attempted to avoid Allied captivity. The wounded man on the stretcher was not an important Nazi, but William Joyce (better known as "Lord Haw-Haw") was sufficiently hated for his propaganda to be tried by the British for treason. He was executed on January 3, 1946, a judgement which reflected his notoriety rather than his guilt.

Below: The German conquests of the first half of the war had enabled several top Nazis to indulge their aesthetic tastes. These are just some of the collection of treasures at Reichmarshall Goering's Königsee home. Goering was a looter on a grand scale, but his tastes in this area were refined – three of the paintings the Allies discovered were Rembrandts.

Above: Hela Goldstein, a Polish Jew, speaks to the world on Movienews from Belsen – behind her a pit filled with human corpses. Pictures like this ensured that in most Western states, Zionist aspirations for a Jewish state in Palestine received strong popular backing and support.

Above: Members of the British Royal Army Medical Corps (RAMC) helping to clean up the concentration camp at Bergen-Belsen. Most of the German camp staff had fled as the Allied forces approached – accelerating the death rate. When the RAMC started to help the victims, they estimated a further 10,000 would die; some died of typhoid, others of accumulated brutal abuse – even the decent food provided by the liberators killed those whose bodies were used to semi-starvation.

Left: As undeniable proof of the Nazi genocide the Allies filmed the camps they liberated, and these films not only convinced their own people that the Holocaust was real, but also provided shocking viewing for the defeated Germans. As part of a process of de-Nazification many Germans were forced to watch these films – during the war many Germans preferred to remain ignorant of the crimes of their regime.

Above: The Allies captured most of the surviving leading figures of the Nazi regime, and tried them in front of the International Military Tribunal in Nuremberg. The defendants, all flanked by white helmeted military police, were given six months to prepare their defence and had legal representation. In stark contrast to the criminality of Nazi occupation, this trial, for all its flaws, was a genuine legal process.

Below: The Nuremberg defendants reacted very differently to the charges; some, such as Balder von Shirach (back row, second right) admitted the horror of their crimes; the military men and conservative politicians refused to admit their complicity; others seemed mentally confused, notably Rudolf Hess (front row, second right); Goering (front row, first right) alone was lucid and defiant. He was to take poison and cheat the gallows.

Above: The International Military Tribunal was made up of judges from France, the USA, Great Britain and the USSR. Altogether 12 defendants were sentenced to death (including an absent Martin Bormann), 7 received prison sentences and 3 were acquitted; clearly the court had not presumed guilt.

The cost of the war in Europe was immense and, particularly in Eastern Europe, the fighting was so disruptive that casualty figures are at best an educated guess. Numerically the USSR suffered more casualties than any other belligerent, and the latest estimate suggests the Soviet population was 30 to 40 million less in 1945 as a result of the war. Proportionally, Poland was probably the most dramatic victim of World War II with 5.4 million dead. Casualties in Western Europe were not so dramatic, but Britain suffered 485,000 dead, and France had over 500,000 fatal casualties.

Germany was the greatest Axis sufferer – some experts assess their losses as nearly 7.4 million dead, but the Italians – reluctant belligerents from their entry into the war – suffered 410,000 dead, and Hungary – a minor Axis ally – had 400,000 military dead alone. The physical destruction was also horrendous, and in the parts of the USSR occupied by Germany half the urban dwellings and three quarters of rural dwellings were in ruins in 1945. Destruction on this scale could only be inflicted by mobilising the power of industrial economies, and it was the USA's efforts in

this respect that really dwarfed all other belligerents. By 1945 it had built 300,000 aircraft alone; at the Ford factory at Willow Run one B-24 bomber was produced every 63 minutes. Despite the USA only partially mobilising its economy it devoted $286 billion of production to the war, and via the "Lend Lease" scheme America functioned as the "arsenal of democracy". It was not to be long before this immense industrial potential was once more harnessed for war, but thankfully the Cold War was to be won and lost on the factory floor rather than the battlefield.